LIVING IN ONE ROOM

LIVING IN ONE ROOM

JON NAAR & MOLLY SIPLE

PHOTOGRAPHED BY JON NAAR

VINTAGE BOOKS
A DIVISION OF RANDOM HOUSE
NEW YORK

FIRST VINTAGE BOOKS EDITION November 1976

Library of Congress Cataloging in Publication Data

Naar, Jon.
  Living in one room.

  1. Apartments. 2. Interior decoration. I. Siple,
Molly, joint author. II. Title.
[NK2195.A6N22 1976]   747′.8′831   76-10579
ISBN 0-394-72076-8 pbk.
Design: Robert Aulicino
Manufactured in the United States of America

For Regi Goldberg

CONTENTS

INTRODUCTION

EIGHT ONE-ROOM ENVIRONMENTS
1

ORGANIZING YOUR SPACE
19

SLEEPING
39

COOKING
57

SITTING. EATING. ENTERTAINING
71

WORKING AT HOME
95

SHARING YOUR SPACE WITH PETS AND PLANTS
107

STORAGE
119

PERSONAL TEXTURE
131

APPENDIX
146

INTRODUCTION

More and more people are living in one-room spaces these days, not always by choice. Sharply increased living costs, especially in the cities, have made roomier accommodations almost prohibitive, and what began as making do has become, for many, a new lifestyle. Today, not only young people starting out on their own and old people on retirement pay, but business people, self-employed artisans and professionals— including a surprisingly large number of architects and designers—eat, sleep, entertain and often work in one-room situations.

If you have limited space, if your walls need pushing out, literally or figuratively, you may find it helpful to see how others are coping with these problems. In the pages that follow we show a wide range of one-room situations that offer a number of ideas and suggestions to make one-room living more enjoyable.

Some of the suggestions are so simple anyone can do them. Others may require outside help in carpentry or minor construction. Obviously, the extent of your investment in your one room will depend on how much money you have and how long you plan to stay there. But if you have been thinking of saving every penny for a move to larger space, reconsider your decision. Perhaps for less money you can create a better environment where you are and save on moving costs and extra rent. It is at any rate with such a view in mind that this book is presented.

1

EIGHT
ONE-ROOM
ENVIRONMENTS

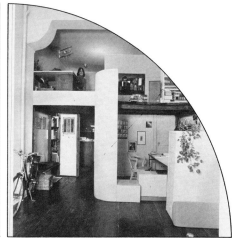

Before tackling the specifics of one-room living, we invite you on a "house tour" of eight special one-room spaces. As you will see, they and their occupants—five women, four men, including a couple—differ widely. The smallest apartment measures twelve by fifteen feet, the largest fifteen by twenty-five feet. Six of the rooms were rectangular (including one L-shaped) and two square. Only one had a ceiling over twelve feet high, and it had a loft built in. Two others had platforms added. All of them show what can be accomplished by intelligent use of space, ingenuity and personal taste, plus the special magic that comes from a blend of all these elements. Most were done on modest budgets.

None of the interiors shown in this section is "decorated" in the traditional sense. The basic arrangement of space and furnishing has been worked out individually by the people who live in the rooms to suit their own needs and interests. Several of the occupants are designers themselves; some others got professional help. Most of them did their own construction, using materials from primary sources such as hardware stores and lumberyards. Even when structural changes were made, the work was kept simple.

Common to these otherwise very different environments are the defining of the main activity areas and the limiting of them, usually to not more than three functions. Another distinctive and important feature of every situation is the leaving or the creating of a "free zone." However small this free space is, it serves an important double purpose—it adds a dimension of roominess at all times and offers space for special and unforeseen activities when the occasion arises.

Although none of them may fit your individual needs, each in its way embodies an idea or a principle that can be adapted to other requirements. Seen as a group, these apartments will, we hope, encourage you to organize your own space more creatively and more enjoyably.

The design of Donald Cromley's small (thirteen by twenty-three feet) basement apartment shows his background and experience as an architect. Each area is worked out functionally—the bed (striped blanket in right foreground) is also used for seating, as are the stacked Aalto stools. Running along the wall to the left is a shelf fifteen feet long and sixteen inches wide that accommodates books and hi-fi equipment, provides space for working and, near the kitchen, preparing food. Underneath the shelf are two pull-out beds for Cromley's twin children who visit on weekends. His free-standing drafting table is anchored to a bookshelf wall unit built from industrial shelving, available at office supply stores. Because the room is small, Cromley decided to make its proportions more horizontal so that it would appear larger than it actually is. He says he would have liked to lower the seven-and-a-half-foot ceiling, but this was not physically possible. Instead he painted it (and an eighteen-inch strip on the walls below) yellow. He painted the rear wall, which divides the main area from the kitchen and bath, blue so that it appears to be an *object* placed within the room past which the white wall to the left runs, extending the space visually.

2 The combination of white walls, natural daylight and well-defined areas for different activities gives the fifteen-foot-square apartment of illustrator Barbara Samuels a warm, light feeling. The bed, placed along the wall, has a sense of privacy, as if it were in an alcove. The cooking area is housed in the base of a space divider that runs across the width of the apartment and helps to define the bed and work areas, as does the bare wood floor. The apartment was designed with the help of architect Tod Williams.

Viewed from the bed, the work area of the
Samuels apartment, lit by natural light from
the window, appears to be isolated, even
though the rocking chair in the music area
is only inches away from the worktable. (For
another view of this apartment, see photograph on cover.)

3 Christopher Duffy, a sociology student, saved considerable space in his twelve-by-fifteen-foot room by putting a large double bed underneath a raised dining/working platform, which he built for under $100. Careful planning enables the bed to slide out in the area in front of the fireplace, which is left free when the armchair is placed on the platform.

4 This L-shaped apartment, twelve by twenty-three feet, is shared by Norman and Christina Diekman. When they married, they considered moving to a larger place but decided not to exchange the wonderful view and nice neighbors for an extra bedroom. The sleeping area is in the left corner near the window, beneath what was an awkward beam and column that was framed out as a niche. The long, narrow table doubles for business meetings with designer Norman's clients and for meals prepared by gourmet cook Christina. (For details, see photographs 47 and 54.)

5 A three-level loft is the dominant feature in architect Regi Goldberg's apartment. She designed it for working (upper left), sleeping (behind the drawing table), with a direct pass-through opening down to the kitchen for breakfast in bed, and as a library (upper right). The ladder is hidden in the round storage wall, and on the lower level there is a second work area. Goldberg's loft, which she built herself at a cost of under $150, is not connected to the walls; it is completely bolted and screwed together and can be removed if she leaves the apartment. It has been changed three times to reflect changes in the room's activities. The open space beyond the loft (see photograph 45) is only fifteen feet square, but it seems larger because of the low furnishings and the high ceiling.

7 In the apartment Joseph Durso designed for fashion designer Susan Klevorick, each of the three levels performs at least two functions: eating/working at the top, near the kitchen and storage areas; sleeping/lounging (and working) in the middle; and sitting/entertaining at the bottom, which has the highest ceiling. As the levels go up, the ceiling gets lower, and the space becomes more intimate.

13

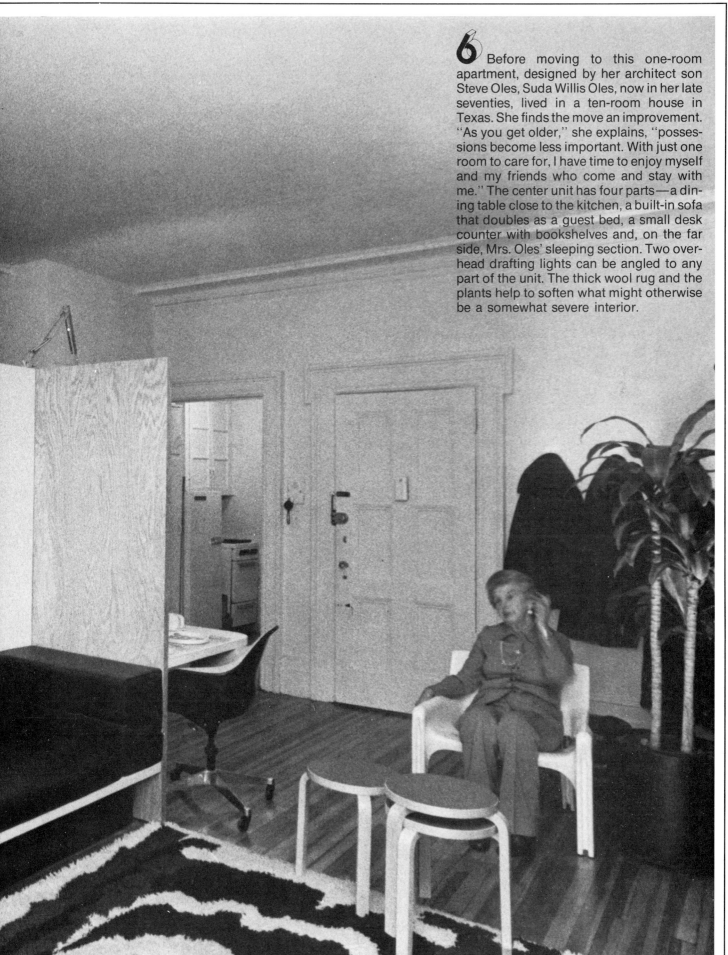

6 Before moving to this one-room apartment, designed by her architect son Steve Oles, Suda Willis Oles, now in her late seventies, lived in a ten-room house in Texas. She finds the move an improvement. "As you get older," she explains, "possessions become less important. With just one room to care for, I have time to enjoy myself and my friends who come and stay with me." The center unit has four parts—a dining table close to the kitchen, a built-in sofa that doubles as a guest bed, a small desk counter with bookshelves and, on the far side, Mrs. Oles' sleeping section. Two overhead drafting lights can be angled to any part of the unit. The thick wool rug and the plants help to soften what might otherwise be a somewhat severe interior.

8 Sculptor-designer Michael Kalil's studio measures twelve by twenty-three feet and is dominated by a three-by-fourteen-and-a-half-foot black vinyl-covered table running down the middle of the room. This table, which is strongly constructed, is used for working, eating, displaying artworks and books, and sleeping (on a mat). Underneath is a library and storage unit. In a niche on the right is a mirror (in which Kalil is seen), which extends the space and in effect doubles the window area. (For another view of this remarkable environment, see photograph 79).

ORGANIZING YOUR SPACE

In writing and illustrating this book, we interviewed over a hundred people, asking them for suggestions, based on their own experience, of how best to plan and organize a one-room apartment on a relatively modest budget. While there was wide variation in details, there was almost complete agreement on basic principles. Whether you are moving into a one-room situation for the first time, or rearranging one you already have, the following guidelines should get you off to a good start. All the points raised are discussed in greater detail in the sections that follow.

Face the Space: See and feel your room as a world that can satisfy your needs and wishes, from the most basic to the most esoteric. Measure your floor area, ceiling height and walls; find out if any of the latter can be moved or changed (you'll need expert help here). See which structural features you can use. For example, alcoves, niches, closets, columns and windows can all work to your benefit, especially in tight quarters. (See photograph 4.)

Decide Your Priorities: How important to you is privacy? Do you have or want a roommate? How often do you entertain or work at home? List your main preferences in living arrangements and see how you can work them into the space you have.

Define Your Activities: What you do at home and how you do it determine the solutions to your space problems. If you like privacy when you sleep, your sleep area has to be secluded. Gourmet cooks need kitchen facilities that everyday cooks do not. If you teach modern dance or exercises in your live-in studio, your floor area has to be left free and might take up as much as 80 percent of the total space. Obviously, this will affect the remaining area left over for sleeping, eating, entertaining and other activities. (See photographs 10 and 11.)

21

9 As you enter the apartment of designer William Machado, you see light-colored, non-patterned fabrics and textures on the floor and walls; table and chairs grouped for entertaining friends and business meetings (Machado works at home, see photograph 60); a wall of shelves lined with books, pictures, records and hi-fi equipment; and, to the rear, the work/sleep area. Through a narrow vertical slit cut in the center partition one glimpses Machado at his worktable by the arched window. Back in the main area, the artworks partly screened by the plants lend a sense of mystery deepened by the pendulum-like stone sculpture of Michael Kalil.

10 Kas Zapkus is an artist, and his loft studio leaves no doubt where his priorities are, from the painting in progress on the floor in the foreground to the framed canvas face to the wall on the left and another painting hanging above the sleeping area at the top center. (For a closer view of this area, see photograph 21). Dividing the sleeping area from the rest of the room are an antique desk and file cabinets topped by plants. The long table, which is on casters, is used for eating and as a work surface for silk screening. Chairs are lightweight so they can be moved easily when more floor space is needed. The hi-fi speaker is placed high in a ceiling corner for excellent sound reproduction.

The one-room live-in studio of modern-dance teacher Georgette Schneer is in some ways a counterpart of Zapkus' loft because it, too, devotes about three-quarters of its space to work. Yet the living areas are quite different. Schneer's own corner is protected by a movable screen, and the interior is a warm tapestry of personal fabrics, artifacts and furnishings. Even though she opens this area as a dressing room for students, it remains a beautiful private interior. (For a close-up, see photograph 24.)

12 The built-in one-room environment designed and inhabited by architect George Ranalli crisply etches the different activity areas. As you enter at the left rear, the low ceiling space suggests mystery, which suddenly opens into a dazzling white main interior. In the center, in a kind of *baldacchino,* is the eating section, whose hard-edged severity is softened by the rose glow of a circular neon light. The benches contain storage space. Above is the sleeping loft, reached by a pyramid-shaped stairway with bookshelves recessed on the left side. To the right is Ranalli's studio, a drafting unit backed by bookshelves for reference materials and supplies. The floor is bare wood, stained dark.

Develop Activity Areas for different needs. Sleeping, eating and sitting are, of course, the basic ones. Relate these to other activities and to each other. Sleeping/sitting can go together, if you don't mind people sitting on your bed. Other combinations are cooking/eating, eating/entertaining, sitting/entertaining. Some don't normally go together, e.g., working/sleeping. But there are exceptions. Work out your own permutations. Look at other people's solutions. (See photographs 1 and 2.)

"Multifunction" is an awkward term for a vital element in making your one-room space work efficiently. By "doubling up," tripling, even quadrupling you can get incredible mileage out of a single area or object. The counter in a kitchen pass-through transforms as if by magic into a drafting table for an architect. (See photographs 55 and 56.) A dramatic night-and-day switch between office and private life is seen in photographs 14 and 15.

Move It Around: When you live in one room, you can't afford to lock yourself in with heavy, fixed objects. Lightweight furnishings and storage units on wheels or casters make your space more flexible. By moving the components around, you can completely change the character of an environment. (See photograph 75.)

Diversify Your Space to offset the closed-in feeling of a single room if it's small or the monotony of a large open room. Use fixed structural features (alcoves, niches, for example) to separate smaller areas from larger ones within the overall space. Columns and posts can break up space vertically, as can the different levels created by pits, platforms and lofts. (See photographs 3, 5, 7, and 73.) Ceilings can be lowered physically with carpentry or hangings or visually with paint, mirrors and other materials to give an effect of intimacy or to make the space seem larger. Floor surfaces can be varied with rugs (not wall-to-wall carpeting, which unifies the surface, making it seem smaller), wood textures or tiles.

The extra dimension of an outside view and of changing natural light, even at night, is a very important factor in making a one-room space livable over a long period. Wall hangings, bookcases, plants, screens, panels, work equipment and other devices can, with imagination, also give your space variety. (See photograph 18.)

Open Living: When you live in one room, there's not much place to hide. You are permanently on display. Enjoy the lived-in look— kitchens in plain sight, beds that are obviously beds, work areas that look worked in. This does not have to look tacky; it is often beautiful, as many examples in this book show. Keep in mind that organizing your space is a continuous process, never completely finished, reflecting the changes which go on in your life.

Personal Texture is what makes your space yours. Feel free to put on view whatever is important or amusing to you—photographs, artwork, jewelry, hobbies, found objects, clutter. Because personal texture is easier to illustrate than to describe, we have devoted a portfolio of photographs to it as the last section of this book.

Ask for Help: As we have suggested, if extensive carpentry or structural changes seem called for, it is best to consult an expert. More and more architects and interior designers are working on small-space problems and can be hired at hourly rates. If in doubt, get bids from two or three people. If you have no special contact in this field, contact the nearest branch of the American Institute of Architects, the American Society of Interior Designers or the local Yellow Pages.

13 In architect Stephen Potters' remodeled loft studio, there is a clear division of public and private areas. The space is a double cube, a fourteen-by-twenty-eight-foot floor plan with a ceiling height of fourteen feet. The sleeping loft has a storage-room wall to the rear and a parapet to the front with part of the original studio railing set into it. By contrast, the studio space below appears very open. Walls and ceilings are painted white, and furnishings are kept to a minimum. The architectural severity is muted by the large leather sofa, the long Navajo rug and the two circular paintings. The kitchen occupies the low area between the entry and the studio (see also photograph 49).

14 By day this room is the office of John Curran, product developer and designer, where he holds business meetings, makes phone calls, dictates letters and works at the drawing board. Because of the way he works, Curran likes his space to be as flexible as possible. He spends most of his time telephoning from one of the chairs or talking to associates around the low wicker table.

15 After work, Curran opens up the sofa for a night's sleep and an early breakfast before his associates arrive. The transition between work and private life is made easy by the relatively simple furnishings in the room, the plain walls and the bare wood floor combined with the softly diffused light through the window blinds. A slender tree accentuates the height of the room and separates the drawing table from the sleeping area.

16 Every component part in the London attic of consultant/designer Michael Wolff moves. The cotton-covered foam-rubber cushions that can be combined into a bed are also used to sit on around a low coffee table that moves on casters, as do the TV table, the hi-fi speakers (covered in white cotton for visual muting) and the cabinet to the right, which houses records and hi-fi equipment. The entire scene can be cleared in minutes for a party or a business meeting.

17 A very different way to design the interior of an L-shaped room (compare with photograph 4) was worked out by architect Cloud Rich for himself. Here, there is dramatic counterplay between soft (wool rugs, suede and leather on banquette and bed, velvet cushions) and hard (plastic chairs and tables), with a horizontal line of artworks above which a mirrored ceiling creates another dimension. Over the banquette in the alcove, the absence of mirrors leaves a quieter space for conversation and overnight guests.

SLEEPING

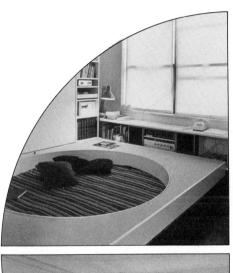

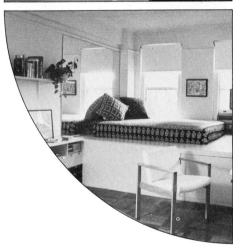

Since you spend roughly one-third of your life in bed, it is logical to give top priority to where and how you want to sleep. Once this problem is solved, your other daily living needs can be dealt with much more easily—especially seating, which requires similar furniture.

Your basic sleeping needs are: space a little larger than you and (if you have one) a sleeping companion; a surface hard enough to support your back; quiet; good ventilation; and as much separation as posssible from other areas of activity, especially if you are sharing your apartment with a roommate. There are a number of possible sleeping arrangements, and you should consider the unusual as well as the more familiar. After all, at Monticello, Thomas Jefferson designed a bed placed in a wall and open to the rooms on either side.

A Mattress or a mattress plus box spring, placed directly on the floor (see photographs 18 and 19), on a platform (see photograph 20), or fitted into a platform (see photograph 22) makes a highly satisfactory bed. If you have children who visit regularly, keep a mattress stored under other furniture, such as a low table or counter, and slide it out across the floor when needed (see photograph 1).

The problem with using a large mattress in a one-room space is that it may look too prominent. To integrate the mattress into the surrounding furniture, cover it and other seating with the same fabric; soften the mattress's appearance with pillows and place it in a prominent position so that it looks as if it were meant to dominate.

A Sofa Bed saves space by providing for both sleeping and sitting and helps your one room look like a living room with no hint of a bed (see photographs 14 and 15). You can have a coffee table in front, even though the sofa bed pulls out, if you stick to small, lightweight tables that can be easily moved.

19 A mattress and bedding placed directly on the floor can have considerable style, as in this Munich apartment of writer Erik Mosel.

18 Architect Susan Green filled in one end of her living space with her bed, mattresses stacked double and covered with inexpensive Indian cotton bedspreads and pillows. The basket of yarn is for knitting while lounging. The hammock supplements the mattresses' functions. If you don't need as much seating space as this, try a single mattress in the corner of the room or along the wall and give it the same treatment.

20 At the window end of this one-room apartment, designed by Dorothea Elman, a wood platform with storage space underneath supports a mattress for sleeping and sitting. At the right is a wood countertop that, when needed as a table, pulls out onto a modular unit which stores wine and other food supplies.

A Private Sleeping Area: If you live with someone with whom you do not sleep, it is essential to provide privacy. There are a number of ways to hide a bed. Stand a screen in front of it. Hang drapery from a frame constructed over it (see photograph 24). Put it in an alcove or at one end of your apartment and block it from view with a pull-down shade.

Lofts are a very practical way of organizing your room, since they use vertical space and leave room underneath for seating, eating, working and storage. If you are unfamiliar with carpentry, a loft may seem like a big project to undertake, but a simple loft can be built in one or two days and will cost less than a sofa bed. Since heat rises, lofts should be open on both sides at the upper sleeping level for better air circulation.

21 This platform bed in the loft of painter Kas Zapkus began with an I-beam (the dark strip along the left side) too heavy to be moved. The platform extends from the I-beam and frames the mattress, which sits on the floor. The mattress is higher than the platform so that a person on the bed will not bump into the frame. Quarter-round moldings edge the platform to eliminate sharp edges. The area is also used for entertaining, reading and storage. Bed linens are kept on the nearby shelves, and books are protected from dust by glass doors in the bookshelves.

22 In the Paris studio apartment of industrial designer Olivier Mourgue, the bed is separated from the main living space by a canvas shade that pulls down for privacy. On the wall are canvas storage bags designed by Mourgue.

The drawback of the sofa bed is that the mattress must be fairly thin and without box springs so that it can fold in half to convert the bed into a sofa. An alternative is to get someone to design a sofa bed in which the sofa back lifts up to reveal a mattress that does not fold, but this is likely to be expensive.

A Day Bed is a mattress fitted with a frame that includes a railing or some sort of raised barrier at the foot and head. Placed against a wall, a day bed converts into a sofa when pillows are put along the wall side and two ends.

A Sleeping Bag is handy for overnight guests, especially children, who like sleeping on the floor. It can be very comfortable if used with a foam mattress (see photograph 27). Both bag and mattress pack into small rolls that can be stored in a closet.

Folding Army Cots which store easily are handy for guests. A well-designed Scandinavian version can be folded and hung on the wall.

Tatami Mats, made from special Japanese grass, are wafer-thin, but their devotees claim that they provide the most orthopedically healthy sleeping. They are very inexpensive and can be recycled as exercise mats if they don't work out for sleeping.

Upholstered Pillows, while not the height of comfort, provide an adequate sleeping surface. By day they can be arranged for seating and by night covered with a fitted sheet.

A Hammock can hang on hooks, one sunk into a window frame, the other into the wall. (See photograph 18.) When not in use, a hammock takes up practically no space and can be unhooked and stored. But make certain it is secure, especially if there will be two of you in it.

23 The upper level of the one-room attic in Berlin designed by Finn Bartels is a loft for sleeping.

24 A garment rack on casters, covered with South Pacific tapa cloth, screens the sleeping area in the corner of dancer Georgette Schneer's studio. When the studio is not being used for dance lessons, the screen is rolled open so that the bed area is more accessible. During lessons, students dress behind the screen and hang their clothes on the rack. The space is further screened by low bookshelves, a pegboard bulletin board and a long tabletop used as a desk. The cloth hanging from the edge of the tabletop conceals an antique cot that can be pulled out for guests. A closer view of the sleeping area full of memorabilia is shown in photograph 84.

25 This seating pit consists of a wooden platform, with a circle cut out of it, which rests on a double mattress. Noa and Eli Attia pull the mattress out from under the platform for overnight guests, and they themselves sleep on a Murphy bed that drops down from the wall behind the platform.

26 In Colonial times some people got privacy in their sleeping area by draping the bed with transparent muslin, and it still works. The space becomes multifunctional with the addition of a portable desktop placed on the bed linen.

27 A twelve-foot-long seating unit in the apartment of Cloud Rich consists of two mattresses stacked on two box springs and placed side by side, making an intimate alcove for entertaining at the far end of an L-shaped room. When Rich's children visit, they spend the night in sleeping bags on the mattresses.

COOKING

Most kitchens in one-room situations are extremely small, and you will have to use all your ingenuity to make yours as efficient as is humanly possible. First, make sure that it meets your individual needs so that you don't waste any space. For example, do you prepare regular meals when you are alone? If so, you will need more equipment than if you normally eat out. If you entertain friends often, you must have sufficient dinnerware as well as larger pots to cook in.

If you cook for many people at a time, you'll need extra storage for large pots. If you don't cook for guests, you can free counter space in your kitchen for work surfaces or as a bar during parties.

The photographs in this chapter suggest a number of ways to increase kitchen storage space inexpensively and attractively, but first you might consider reorganizing your storage. Study the way you use your kitchen and relate your storage to your habits.

Put cooking pots, especially heavy ones, at shoulder height. For extra convenience, store heavy utensils and appliances in a cabinet with a pull-out shelf that takes fifty pounds of weight. You can get these from restaurant equipment supply companies.

Give away duplicate utensils and any that you haven't used in five years.

Use wire shelf-arrangers in cabinets and on open shelving.

Hang small utensils you use most often near the sink. Install a small shelf on the wall near your stove to hold your most often used spices, salt and pepper.

Leave heavy small appliances, like a blender, on counters and shelves.

If you have graduated mixing bowls and regularly use the smallest, keep only this one handy.

Because uncluttered work space seems larger, store foods like rice and cereal in uniform containers. Clean up the clutter around the sink.

28 A kitchen can be beautiful if someone is spending hours there happily cooking, like Bob Propper. Here herbs are at arm's reach in bottles to the right and growing in the window; stacks of regularly used cooking oil, coffee and bouillon cubes are on the counter; cookbooks are one shelf up. The shelving is supported by metal standards and brackets. Packing crates provide open storage and even a knife rack. A stool is kept under the counter for long cooking sessions and eating alone. And a small compact broiler sits to the far right of the counter, a good space saver and very useful for cooking dinner for one or two.

29 A can-wide shelf like this one, which architect David Specter installed in his kitchen, uses only three or four inches of a room's width. Colorful labels transform the storage wall into a display. You can also build narrow shelves inside a cabinet in a U-shape along the sides and across the back.

30 Screens that roll down and freestanding folding screens hide a kitchen that may not be as attractive as the rest of your room. Bamboo screens like this are inexpensive and can be installed easily with a few nails or hung from hooks.

31 Every inch of space is used in this kitchen—metal shelves are locked into standards screwed to the back of the door; there is vertical shelving over the stove, pegboard on the walls, can-wide shelving, a counter for cooking and eating, shelves for cookbooks set into a niche in the wall on the right, and one very high shelf near the ceiling to hold rarely used equipment, with cups hung underneath.

32 A Munich engineer devised this simple open-storage system, using two vertically stacked orange crates. Cup hooks hold mugs, potholders and sundry utensils. Spice and herb jars sit on a small outside side shelf while other containers are stored on top.

33 If you are lucky enough to find a free-standing antique kitchen cabinet, as Pat Green did, you can use it for preparing food, storing supplies, equipment and cookbooks. The shelf above the unit holds dinnerware, and skillets hang from its underside.

34 A wall storage unit that incorporates shelving and a drop-down counter was designed by architect J. Woodson Rainey, Jr. His wife covered it with vinyl and added to the design with a collection of trays, miniature canned goods and gourmet foods.

Take extra bottles and old supermarket receipts off the top of the refrigerator. Put the bottles in the far corner of a shelf and the receipts in an envelope or a covered container.

To add work surface, fit a butcher block with wire handles and lay it across the top of your sink. As you cut and prepare food, let the trimmings drop into the sink, where they can be easily collected to throw out. Or build an extra counter by attaching a shelf to a wall with hinges. The

65

counter can then be kept flat against the wall, held with a hook, and dropped for use.

For long hours of work, get a stool with a back. If you like to stand while you cook, get a small rug.

Good lighting in the kitchen is essential. The ideal place is under the wall cabinets, over the counter. Luminescent light is good because it doesn't cast shadows. Fluorescent light, except when balanced for daylight, drains food of its color so that you can't tell if the broccoli is still green or hopelessly overcooked. Try a clip-on, movable spotlight for such eye-straining processes as deveining shrimp and other close work.

35 If your kitchen is open to the room and you want to delineate your cooking area, hang a flag from the ceiling and place a counter in front. Susan Green uses a stainless-steel restaurant storage unit on casters. A butcher-block top has been added, and the under shelf is used for storage. (For a view of this apartment from the opposite direction, see photograph 18.)

36 Painter Kas Zapkus created this ingenious dish drainer to drip water directly into the sink, via a shaped rubber mat, saving valuable space and eliminating the bother of sponging the counter.

37 A narrow galley kitchen can be highly efficient in a small-space situation because everything is at arm's reach. A mirror under the cabinet on the right makes the kitchen look wider. Tod Williams also installed a small-scale, 110-volt, fan-powered oven in the wall on the left. To the rear is a children's sleep and play loft that can be seen through the opening over the kitchen door.

SITTING, EATING, ENTERTAINING

When you are alone in your one room, there is no problem finding a place to sit or eat. For two or three visitors, you can probably make do with the seating you have and a regular table (see photograph 9). Having more people, especially for a meal, requires a certain amount of planning. There are several options for expanded seating:

The floor can be quite comfortable if you have a thick rug or carpet.

Pillows placed on the floor or leaned against the wall for back support appeal to many people. A single large flat pillow can be used for sitting cross-legged at a low table (see photographs 38 and 39).

Lightweight chairs, stools and modular units that combine like building blocks make for flexible seating arrangements (see photographs 40 and 41).

Folding and stacking chairs are good space savers and can be stored either in plain sight or in a closet. Some chairs can also hang from hooks (see photographs 46, 47, 48 and 51).

Platforms organize seating vertically, sometimes with a series of rising ledges. However, because they are fixed, they cannot be easily regrouped for changing needs (see photograph 42).

Built-in seating units can be integrated with the structure of your room, filling otherwise hard-to-use space like that in front of a window or a corner (see photograph 43).

Choose seating that is comfortable and put your own needs ahead of those who will use it only occasionally. If you are tall, you need deep seats to accommodate the length of your legs, shallower seats if you are short. The height of your seating should also be scaled to the height of tables and counters.

38 Olivier Mourgue loves Japan, and in his own studio apartment in Paris he and his wife Christina sit on pillows on the floor for all their meals. The only "real" chairs they use in this space are Mourgue's humanoid Bouloums, made of molded plywood and covered with stretch fabric. They are surprisingly comfortable and can be moved easily. The wonderful kite display on the wall adds color and pattern.

To increase your eating facilities, consider drop-down, pull-out and expanding tables; these give you an eating surface that takes up very little room when not in use. Trays and folding tray tables permit you to eat in different sections of your room as the spirit moves you. Other more ingenious solutions to the eating problem are illustrated in this chapter (see photographs 47, 48, 50).

Placing your table just outside the kitchen saves steps serving and clearing; before meals you can use the surface to prepare the food (see photograph 49). If your table is a distance from the kitchen, use a bookshelf or small table near the dining table as a buffet to hold casseroles and dishes, after-dinner coffee, dessert.

Clearing the table after a meal will take you from your guests for a few minutes, but this is better than looking at dirty dishes for the rest of the evening. Or, you can try dimming the light in the eating area so that the table can hardly be seen.

When you are having a party in a one-room apartment, you have to be well organized ahead of time. If you think you will need more chairs, borrow some. If you want to see a large number of your friends during an evening, stagger the hours that you invite them. Rather than a sit-down meal, serve a one-course buffet so that you don't have to keep bringing out different foods and collecting used plates. Place the serving dishes in at least two places so that guests don't all crowd in one spot. Leave a tray handy for dirty dishes and remove it periodically. Have plenty of small side tables, stools or overturned baskets that guests can use as dining tables. Serve food that doesn't need cutting, and, if it is to be eaten with the hands, make certain it isn't the kind that will crumble and spill on the floor. When your guests arrive, hang coats in the bathroom on hangers hooked over the shower curtain rod instead of in a cramped closet. And make sure a window stays

39 Pillows are comfortable to sit on for chess playing and good conversation in architect David Evan Glasser's apartment. The textured fabrics against a white wall help to diversify the space.

open throughout the party so that the room doesn't overheat from having too many people in it.

Although most entertaining involves food and drink, some people give more emphasis to other activities like card playing, backgammon, slide shows, listening to music, dancing and just good conversation. In such cases, arrange your seating and table to suit the entertainment you have in mind and keep the refreshments limited to snacks and drinks.

40 Plastic chairs are light and can be moved to the table for eating, to a desk for work or arranged for conversation wherever it happens in Cloud Rich's apartment. Some guidelines for a conversation group: a comfortable talking distance between two people is five and a half feet, from nose to nose. Most people prefer to talk to someone sitting at a right angle to them rather than across from each other or side by side; a sofa for three is rarely used by three people at once, because it is hard to talk that way.

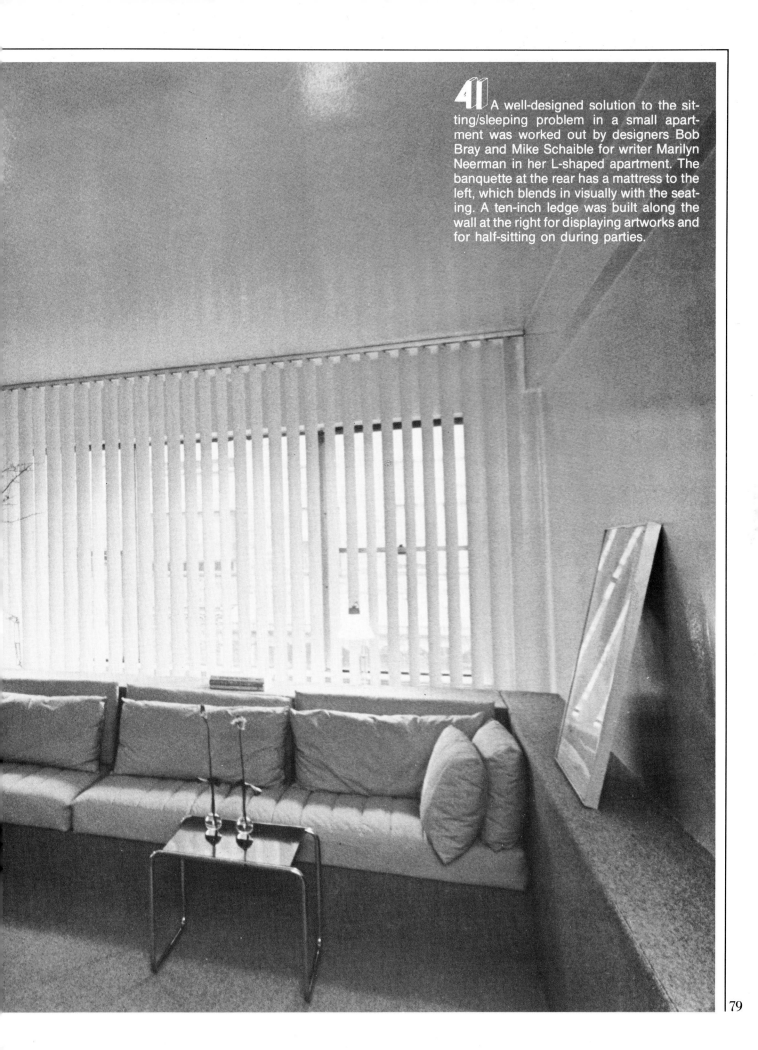

41 A well-designed solution to the sitting/sleeping problem in a small apartment was worked out by designers Bob Bray and Mike Schaible for writer Marilyn Neerman in her L-shaped apartment. The banquette at the rear has a mattress to the left, which blends in visually with the seating. A ten-inch ledge was built along the wall at the right for displaying artworks and for half-sitting on during parties.

42 A three-level conversation corner of wood platforms covered with carpet and pillows was designed by Israeli architect Ari Bahat with the idea of dividing the seating space in the same way that sofas and armchairs do. At a large party, guests can also sit on the carpeted floor on pillows. These units are inexpensive and easy to clean with a vacuum.

43 Compact, built-in seating makes an L-shaped arrangement in architect Tod Williams' living area. The foam pillows lift up for convenient storage. At the left, above the seats, is Tod's sleeping area. A small Navajo weaving is placed on alternate pillows for textural variety.

44 The cantilevered table in author Peter Benchley's apartment designed by architect J. Woodson Rainey, Jr., folds into the wall cabinet. It is used alternately as a desk and as an eating surface one step from the open-wall kitchen. The platform, steps and long narrow table, all made with oak flooring, perform numerous functions as seating, a work surface and an area divider. The wooden floor ends in a diagonal that makes the room look deeper than it is. The windows are covered with semi-opaque sliding glass panels, acid-etched with architectural plans. To let in as much light as possible, no further window covering is used.

45 In the main area of her loft/studio, which looks larger than the fifteen-by-fifteen feet it is because of the high white walls and the low furnishings, Regi Goldberg enjoys brunch with two of her architectural students. For larger groups she uses the low seating area to the left (which doubles for overnight guests), supplemented by pillows on the floor. When entertaining more formally she rearranges her downstairs work area to seat eight people comfortably.

46 A cantilevered table near the kitchen locks into the irregular entrance wall of architect J. Woodson Rainey, Jr.'s apartment. Low chairs tuck under the surface to free walking space.

47 The dining table in the apartment of Christina and Norman Diekman is only twenty-three inches wide, but it can accommodate at least four people comfortably when the settings are staggered. A by-product of the slim dimensions is that guests sit close to each other and enjoy an intimate atmosphere. To make every inch of a dining table count, here are some minimum dimensions: elbow room, two feet two inches of table length per person; depth of a place setting, fifteen inches. The standard height for a dining table is about twenty-eight inches, but you may need a lower table that better matches the low, multipurpose chairs you are probably using.

48 The two narrow tables against the wall push together to make a table for four in the apartment of architect John Davison Allen. A celebrated cook, he likes to give buffet dinner parties for twenty, served from these tables lined against the wall. Allen's apartment includes a terrace seen through the glass door. Even in winter when the terrace is not used, the view of outside space makes the apartment feel larger. For another view of this room and of the kitchen, see photographs 55, 56, and 73.

49 The dining table is conveniently near the kitchen in architect Stephen Potters' loft in the low area between foyer and main studio. Oak cabinets and open shelves enclose sink, stove and refrigerator in a single, compact unit.

50 The drafting table and office desk convert to buffet tables in John Curran's apartment/office (also shown in photographs 14 and 15).

51 The built-in and platform seating in the apartment of architect Beppe Zambonini and his wife, Maria, predetermines where some people will sit at a party. The fixed seating units are supplemented with pillows and chairs that can be moved around the room where needed. The built-ins are placed at angles to the walls to give the L-shaped room more variety. A false column in the middle of the room is covered with mirror to break the monotony of an otherwise conventional space.

WORKING AT HOME

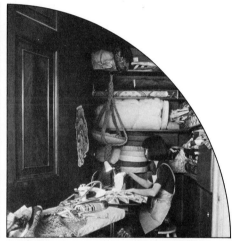

Numerous architects, designers, artists, illustrators, photographers, writers, dressmakers, business executives, agents and consultants work at home in one room, either part or full time. The most common situation is a small "office" with an improvised desk or a work surface on a table or counter, and a file box. If your reference materials and supplies are handy (in a drawer or on a bookshelf) and you don't mind leaving your work out in the open or getting it out every time you start, this method works quite well. For a more elaborate but still inexpensive arrangement, you can line up two standard filing cabinets parallel to each other about eighteen inches apart (for leg room) and cover them with a board, possibly laminated with plastic or covered with linoleum, about five feet long and two and a half feet wide. This will give you a good working surface that can be reused later for meals, games, hobbies, or as a buffet/bar when you have a party.

If your space is really tight, put the file cabinets back to back so that the drawers open sideways, and cover them with a narrow plank (it could be as little as fifteen inches wide, the width of an average file cabinet). This can squeeze into a passageway or fit into a sleeping area, doubling as a work/dressing table or as an area divider.

Some people, obviously not claustrophobes, use closets as darkrooms, sewing centers or private offices. They give you seclusion from the rest of the room's activities (important when there is more than one occupant) and allow you simply to close the door on your work at any moment without having to tidy up (see photograph 53). In certain cases, the door can be replaced with a screen that comes down from the top. Darkrooms can also be constructed in the bathroom.

Alcoves, platforms, lofts and pits also function efficiently as work areas, clearly defined as such and yet integral parts of the total space. They, too, are especially useful when there is more than one occupant in the one room. (See

52 In the loft section of Regi Goldberg's apartment there are at least three working areas. This one is located for privacy under the loft and further screened, to the right and center, by filing cabinets and, to the left, by the side of the storage wall that hides the ladder to the upper level, on the right side of which is a library/music room.

53 Closets come in all sizes, but if you spend much time working in one, make sure it's better lighted than seamstress Dina Carlson's, shown here. If you adapt a closet of your own, paint it white (even if it's going to be a darkroom), improve the lighting and try to put in some ventilation. At photo supply houses, you can get darkroom exhaust fans that work quite efficiently in small spaces.

photographs 4, 7 and 52.)

Work does not always have to be confined to one area. Many people, particularly those who need no equipment except a telephone, a tape recorder, or a pocket calculator, prefer to conduct their business wandering all over the place, selecting whichever spot is most convenient at the time. The better organized your work space is, the better you will work. As you plan and put it together, remember the importance of good light-

54 Designer Norman Diekman solved his work-at-home problem by creating a studio in the alcove of his L-shaped apartment (see also photograph 4). The work area is defined by the structure of the alcove, by the bare wooden floor and partly by the plants. To the rear are three white plywood panels used for displaying fabrics and other materials Diekman is working on. (See photograph 69 for details of Diekman's supply closet.)

55 First, it's a kitchen counter for chef John Davison Allen to prepare a cheese soufflé.

ing, properly placed for the kind of activity you do. Many of the people we photographed used the classic drafting lamp. It is worth the investment of $30 to $40, but be sure to get the original model made by Luxo (photograph 59); the copies look the same but do not work as well mechanically. Aluminum photographic lamps are lightweight and flexible; they clamp on almost anywhere and are inexpensive—under ten dollars in many camera shops and electrical supply stores. Beware of fluorescent lighting; its flicker effect can harm your eyes. Wherever possible use natural light. Seating should also be efficient and comfortable. Because it is such a personal matter, it is impossible to recommend any specific kind. However, if you are working for long periods in a more or less static position, get a seating arrangement (it might not be a chair) that is flexible and gives your back good support.

56 Then, before you can say Julia Child and Frank Lloyd Wright, architect John Davison Allen has whipped out his drafting tabletop from under the counter, swung round the boom lamp from the seating/sleeping pit beyond the kitchen pass-through, and he's ready to work on drawings for a building.

57 Some people like to work at home because they can be near both their reference books and the kitchen, as well as being inspired by the view from the window, which in the studio apartment of Tod Williams looks across 57th Street in New York City.

58 The world of designer/writer Bob Propper is cluttered with personal memorabilia. His bed is to the right rear, underneath a ''window'' to the kitchen. Although there is not much space between each of the activity areas in this room, they seem to work well separately and together. For more detail on the storage wall to the left, see photograph 76.

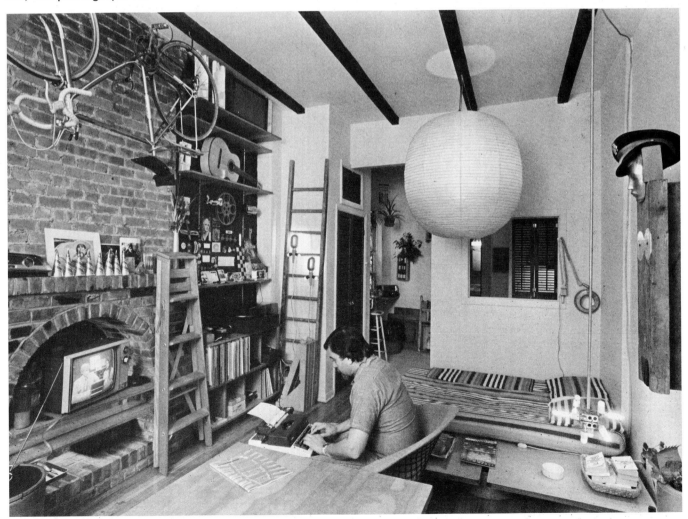

59 A simple way to support a drafting table by using ordinary plumbing pipes painted white was devised by architect J. Woodson Rainey, Jr. The mobile drawer unit is a standard item found in most art supply stores.

60 The worktable in designer William Machado's apartment is large enough for him and an associate. It is located at the window to use the natural light, which is partly diffused by hanging plants and supplemented when necessary by the drafting lamp. In this simply furnished space the low mattress for sleeping does not encroach on the work area.

SHARING YOUR SPACE WITH PETS AND PLANTS

Up to this point we have been concerned with the organization of the one-room environment as it touches on your needs and activities and those of your roommates, guests and children. With regard to the latter, we have restricted our discussion to children as short-term occupants because most psychologists agree that extended sharing of a one-room apartment with a child is psychologically undesirable unless both adult and child have complete privacy. If you have any doubts on this matter, we suggest you consult a more specialized authority. On the other hand, regular brief visits from children of your own or of relatives or friends are enjoyable and can be successfully worked out in a one-room setting.

As to pets, they have lived in harmony with us since time began and make excellent companions for those who are willing to take care of them. Provided they fit into your space, aren't forbidden by your lease, and don't bother the neighbors, there are a number of animals, birds, fish or reptiles you could have. In the situations that we photographed, the overwhelming favorite by a long whisker was the cat. Almost half the places we visited had one or more. They are a good choice because they take up relatively little room, virtually housebreak themselves, and need little attention other than water, regular feeding and a clean litter box. (See photograph 61.)

Small dogs are next in popularity. They require more care than cats and have to be taken out for regular exercise. However, their barking provides a certain amount of security, especially if they are not seen by the would-be intruder. Large dogs don't always make more noise, but they take more looking after and can be a nuisance in small apartments unless their companionship is very important to you. Most big dogs need large, open spaces for exercise, and it is cruel to lock them up all day in a small area.

Birds look attractive if the idea of keeping them in a cage does not distress you. More exotic

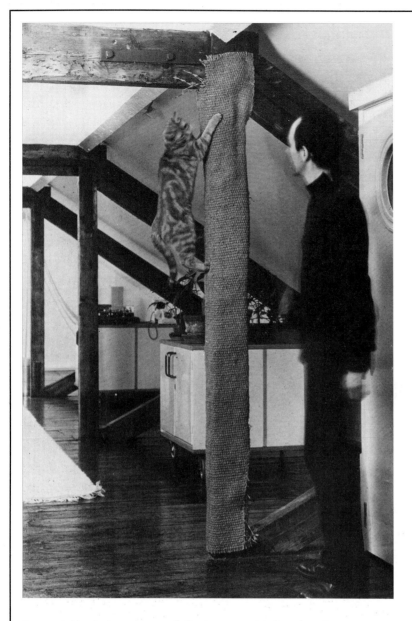

61 By covering a column or pole with burlap you can provide a healthy exercise outlet for a cat in a confined space.

creatures are possible, provided you have the right kind of facilities. Tropical fish are visually interesting as long as you keep their tanks clean and at the right pH and temperature.

Plants also provide your environment with a kind of living presence. They grow and respond to your moods. According to a recent study, they are particularly affected by music. Geraniums, for example, are said to grow faster to the accompaniment of Bach's Brandenburg Concertos (see photograph 63). They are healthy to have around, absorb some odors and toxic elements in the air, and if you treat them right, will produce beauty for you and in some cases—such as herbs—food.

Many of the photographs in this book show how plants serve specific design purposes in small places—to break up an otherwise monotonous area visually, to divide a space, to soften a hard line, to make a room look higher (by having either a tree or a tall slender plant on the floor or a plant hanging from the ceiling) and to diffuse light through a window (see photograph 64). Whatever their function, even if simply to give pleasure, plants, trees and flowers—like animals and human beings—thrive when taken good care of. If you are a plant freak, you will undoubtedly give all the space you can to raising orchids, cacti or a thousand varieties of begonia (see photograph 62). However, for those with more modest ambitions who like to have plants growing in their apartment, here are a few tips on keeping them in their place:

• Save floor space by hanging plants, especially vines and other kinds that grow down, from the ceiling (making sure the wires or ropes are well anchored), from the tops of window recesses, from room dividers—in fact, from anywhere you can screw in a hook sturdy enough to hold the weight of the pot and plant.

• Place taller, wide-spreading plants or trees (five or six feet high) on low tables or pedestal bases so that their widest spread will take up space near the ceiling rather than at eye level.

• Fill windowsills with small pots of plants in soil, or with bottles and jars for those that grow in water. This diffuses the light, and if you use clear plastic pots, the translucency catching the changing light adds a sparkling quality to your space.

• Put plants on glass or clear plastic shelves across windows (see photograph 65).

• Use outside window ledges, balconies or fire escapes for your pots and boxes, but make sure

they are secure (in case of wind) and not in anyone's way.

- Miniature citrus and miniature roses flourish on bright windowsills (or under strong fluorescents) and give off wonderful fragrance.

- Opinion is divided on special "grow" lights for plants, but ordinary fluorescents work well if they have full-spectrum lamps for both leaf and flower growth.

- Dried and straw flowers and many dried weeds and grasses are inexpensive (sometimes free if picked in a field) and work well in any kind of interior.

- Many plants, especially ferns, like humidity and grow well in bathrooms, hanging from the

62 Because she is a cactus buff, JoAnn Czekalski, a systems analyst with a large corporation, gives over a large part of her apartment to her plant collection, which coexists symbiotically with her books and her Yorkshire terrier.

shower curtain rod (see photograph 67), around the tub (see photograph 66) or on shelves.

• If you have a potted tree, use the area around its base for a built-in table.

• Above all, if your plants are doing well, stick with the kind of care you are giving them.

63 Plants respond favorably to the charms of music, especially the live recorder playing in David Evan Glasser's library corner.

65 Herbs grow on glass shelves installed across a kitchen window where pears are also set out to ripen.

64 Ivy vines filter the light and provide a counterpoint to the dramatic architecture in Ward Bennett's penthouse studio.

66 In this bathroom, plants are seen everywhere, even in the prints on the wall at the rear.

67 Many plants thrive in the humidity of a bathroom and, as shown here, can hang in pots from the shower curtain railing.

8

STORAGE

Storage supports every aspect of one-room living. If well planned, it more than almost anything else can make your space work more efficiently. For instance, store objects near where you use them, tableware near where you eat, blankets close to the bed in winter, away in summer.

If you want your room to look uncluttered, cut down your possessions by throwing away everything you don't need and storing most of what's left in closets and drawers. For examples, see the photograph of the apartment designed by John Saladino (see photograph 80) which makes the most of clean surfaces; see also the Barbara Samuels' apartment on the cover.

There's also nothing wrong with having your possessions in the open. The work space of Mimi Lobell (see photograph 77) is an enthusiastic display of books, knitting materials, a favorite hat, a collection of perfume bottles, records—storage that personalizes the space. Open storage is a great space-saver. Start by putting your more interesting belongings on display on shelves and walls. If you don't have enough shelves, you can build more inexpensively by stacking boards on bricks (see photograph 74) or using standards and brackets to hold shelves on the wall or door (see photograph 31).

If you own more non-displayable objects than your closets will hold, try to find other out-of-the-way places to keep them. Instead of investing in a space-consuming chest of drawers, store your belongings under the sofa in attractive containers, or exposed under a table as Michael Kalil did (see photograph 8). Build a shelf high on a wall, out of normal eye-range but not out of reach with a step-ladder. Add a shelf to an unused closet wall—and then install a light so you can see what you have.

You should also make storage do more than just store, so that it will doubly merit the space it fills. Use a bookshelf to divide your room. Put cabinets at the head of your bed and use them as a headboard. Use low cabinets, chests and hampers for seats or tables.

68 Here is an assortment of open storage—antique purses hung on nails in the wall, an open cabinet over the sitting/sleeping mattress, a shelf built into the space in front of the window to hold TV and magazines. A closed basket on the floor contains knitting yarn, and an open basket holds more magazines. The mattress is covered with fabric, topped with colorful pillows and set on a very low platform.

69 Norman Diekman's drafting supplies, pens, swatches of fabric and files are stored in what he calls his "vertical toolbox," just a step from where they will be used, at the drafting table in the next room. (See also photograph 54.)

70 Wicker cases slide conveniently out of the way under the sofa, and a much larger wicker trunk acts as an end table.

71 This setting in the apartment of business executive/designer Pat Green has storage space for extra blankets, ski equipment and other very bulky items; one need only remove the pillows and lift up the wood tops. The sides are faced with split logs that can't be damaged by the five cats and a dog.

72 A hanger and a nail can provide quickly improvised storage and display; in Ari Bahat's apartment they are used to show off a piece of batik silk and store umbrellas.

73 The low cabinet unit which divides the eating area of John Davison Allen's apartment from the sitting/sleeping pit is made from an old cabinet with very narrow shelves and two painted wooden chests. A record player is kept on the top of the divider, and records are stored in the center cabinet beneath. Open shelving with a counter on top also divides the sitting/sleeping area from the kitchen.

74 Wood boards stacked on concrete building blocks provide an ingenious shelving system in publisher/printer Michael Schacht's apartment. The addition of numbers that count the shelves, spare plumbing parts that act as book ends, and a toy train that stretches across the top shelf make ordinary storage into a display.

75 Everything rolls in this corner of Michael Wolff's London attic. Wheels made for industrial use are attached to the mirror, the storage cabinet and the clothing rack. Clothes and shoes hang in closed bags where they will not collect dust.

76 The organized clutter in Bob Propper's apartment is a striking use of storage as display.

PERSONAL TEXTURE

At the core of any arrangement of walls, floor, ceiling and what goes in between, especially in a one-room situation, there is the human element. However efficiently you have dealt with the problems of fitting your needs and activities into the allotted space, it cannot come to life unless you add your own touch.

The photographs in this section show how a variety of creative people have satisfied their requirements and tastes:

- Because she is the person she is, Mimi Lobell created a strikingly warm and feminine cosmos in which to write, study, and be alone.
- For her home environment Fern Mallis fashioned a space that is carefully proportioned, artfully lighted and eminently self-contained.
- Michael Kalil searches for the essence of form, color and function and so imbues his space with a rare, spiritual quality.
- The one-room apartment was designed as a *pied-à-terre* for a bachelor.
- Susan Green's skylit room, festively hung with flag, kite, hammock and plants, has an unself-conscious yet unmistakable harmony.
- Muralist Arthur Long has surrounded himself with an abundance of *chatchkas* that delight his appreciative eyes and those of his guests.
- Graham Brown, actor and photographer, does not consider himself adept at decorating, yet his one room shows style and personal expression.
- In the corner of her dance studio Georgette Schneer composed a sanctuary using fabrics, chairs and objects of special meaning to her.
- Personal memorabilia and clutter do not impede the culinary efficiency in Syl and Barbara Labrot's loft.
- A sense of humor is put to practical use by Michael Schacht in numbering the security system on his front door.

We hope that the solutions devised by the people photographed in this book will inspire you not to imitate them but to feel free to be yourself.

79 Michael Kalil sculptor/designer

78 Fern Mallis fashion coordinator

83 Graham Brown   actor

84 Georgette Schneer   dancer

85 Syl and Barbara Labrot
photographers/graphic designers

Michael Schacht printer/publisher

APPENDIX

SOURCES OF MATERIALS, PRODUCTS AND SUPPLIES

Access to materials, products and supplies varies widely from location to location. There are, however, a number of general sources that could be useful in the organizing of your one-room space. In general, shopping at these sources will be less expensive than at conventional department and furniture stores. The following list is not comprehensive but will give you an idea of what items can be found—sometimes in unexpected and out-of-the-way places.

Lumber suppliers are the logical place to start if you are remodeling or building. Frequently a lumberyard will cut small orders to specification. In addition to wood materials, they stock everything from nails to finished cabinets.

Hardware stores are indispensable and most carry such items as standards and brackets, chains for hanging plants, sliding-door tracks, closet rods, table legs, casters, hinges and pegboard.

Unfinished-furniture stores carry cabinets, bookcases, desks, beds, foam rubber and other items that can be used alone or incorporated into built-in units (see photograph 73).

Houseware stores offer primarily finished products—cabinets, containers of all kinds, garment bags, shoe racks, stepladders, mirrored tile, linoleum, carpet squares, hanging shelves for bathrooms, drawer dividers and shelf arrangers.

Paint stores often sell, in addition to paint, other useful supplies otherwise found in houseware and hardware outlets.

146

Office supply stores are an excellent source for filing cabinets, desks, stools, chairs, lamps, compact refrigerators and industrial shelving, as seen in photographs 1 and 47.

Art supply dealers carry a range of drafting products, including tables, lamps, chairs, rice paper for shoji screens, as well as picture frames, easels and storage units such as the mobile organizer seen in photograph 59.

Army and Navy surplus outlets will provide you with hammocks, footlockers, sleeping bags, blankets and folding cots.

Camping equipment stores cover much the same ground as Army and Navy stores, with particularly good compact-looking equipment and utensils, air mattresses, sleeping bags, folding seats and cots.

Boating supply houses and marine hardware stores furnish well-designed, compact products, materials and finished units such as toilets, refrigerators, stairways (see photograph 37) and galley kitchens that work in any kind of tight space on land as well as on water.

Kitchen appliance manufacturers sometimes specialize in efficiency and small-scale stoves, refrigerators, sinks, cabinets and counters.

Restaurant supply companies offer professional kitchen ranges, stainless-steel storage carts, steam tables (see photograph 35), workbenches and modular shelving.

Hospital equipment manufacturers handle storage carts, surgical lamps and stainless-steel trays and shelving.

Chemical glassware and equipment houses supply glass and ceramic trays, flasks, beakers, containers, dishes, mortars and pestles.

Photographic suppliers and larger camera stores are a good source for lighting of all kinds, especially low-cost aluminum spot and flood reflectors, light stands, and other items that can be adapted for nonphotographic purposes.

Display fixture manufacturers offer shelf systems and garment racks (see photograph 75).

Foam rubber manufacturers are the place to go for mattresses, cushions, bolsters, pillows, carpet underlay and foam blocks for seating/sleeping units.

Plastics outlets offer reflective sheeting, shelf strips, rods, tubes, display stands and many other items in clear or colored plastics.

Thrift shops, Salvation Army, railroad salvage outlets, auctions and tag sales should not be neglected for a very wide variety of inexpensive products and materials.

The town dump and the sidewalk, last but not least, are wonderful places to find possibly just about anything you need—free.

About the Authors

Jon Naar is a widely published photographer/writer whose work appears regularly in *The New York Times Magazine, Fortune, Elle* and other publications in this country and Europe. He is the photographer of *The Faith of Graffiti*, 1974, and is currently working on a book of solar-energy houses.

Molly Siple is an editor at *House Beautiful* and has been an editor at *Interior Design* magazine. She has also designed major collections of bedspreads, wall hangings and dinnerware.